GET WELL SOON

Head Lice

Anita Ganeri and

Beatriz Castro

Enslow PUBLISHING

Published in 2025 by Enslow Publishing, LLC
2544 Clinton Street
Buffalo, NY 14224

First published in Great Britain in 2023 by Hodder & Stoughton

Series editor: Julia Bird
Illustrator: Beatriz Castro
Design: Collaborate

Manufactured in the United States of America

CPSIA compliance information: Batch #CSENS25: For further information contact Enslow Publishing LLC, New York, New York at 1-800-398-2504.

Please visit our website, www.enslowpublishing.com. For a free color catalog of all our high-quality books, call toll free 1-800-398-2504 or fax 1-877-980-4454.

Cataloging-in-Publication Data

Names: Ganeri, Anita, 1961-. | Castro, Beatriz.
Title: Head lice / by Anita Ganeri and Beatriz Castro.
Description: Buffalo, NY : Enslow Publishing, 2025. | Series: Get well soon
Identifiers: ISBN 9781978538658 (pbk.) | ISBN 9781978538665 (library bound) | ISBN 9781978538672 (ebook)
Subjects: LCSH: Pediculosis--Juvenile literature. | Pediculosis--Treatment--Juvenile literature. | Lice--Juvenile literature.
Classification: LCC RL764.P4 G24 2025 | DDC 616.5'72--dc23

GET WELL SOON

Head Lice

Hi! My name's Poppy and this book is all about the time I got head lice. They don't make you feel sick, but you might feel embarrassed or think people will make fun of you.

Don't worry. Head lice are very common, especially when you're with lots of other children at school. Most people get them at some time. Even my brother!

This book has lots of information and advice about head lice. On the following pages, you can find out:

What are head lice?

How do you catch them?

What can you do to get rid of them?

How can you stop them from coming back?

Head lice are often called nits, after the name for their eggs. You can read more about this on page 13.

It’s Friday morning, and Poppy arrives at school.
It’s assembly today, and she doesn’t want to be late.
On the playground she meets Priya, her best friend.

The girls give each other a hug.

The girls go inside and sit down at their desks. They always sit next to each other. They start chatting about going swimming over the weekend.

Their teacher, Miss Lindsay, comes in and claps her hands.

When the class is quiet, Miss Lindsay takes attendance. The children raise their hands as she reads out their names.

Poppy raises her hand. Then she starts scratching her head. It's SO itchy.

Priya puts her hand up. Then she starts scratching her head too.

Miss Lindsay finishes taking attendance. She notices the girls scratching their heads.

But there isn't time to say anything now. They have gym class this morning and they need to get changed.

After lunch, the children go into the school hall. There's a lot of chattering and whispering. Suddenly, everyone goes quiet. The principal, Mrs. Chapman, comes in with Mr. Wilkins, the assistant principal.

Poppy's head is still itching. She gives it a quick scratch. Then another. Next to her, Priya does the same.

Mr. Wilkins tells the children that Mrs. Chapman wants to talk to them about nits. He asks them if they know what nits are. A few children raise their hands.

Mr. Wilkins hands the talk over to Mrs. Chapman.

Mrs. Chapman shows the children a big poster.

SOME NOT-SO-NICE FACTS ABOUT NITS ...

- Nits are the empty egg cases of tiny insects called head lice.
- Head lice can live on your hair, close to your scalp.
- They bite your skin and feed on your blood.
- Adult lice are only the size of sesame seeds.

- Head lice lay their eggs on your hair. The eggs take ten days to hatch.
- When the baby lice crawl out, they leave their white egg cases behind.

The school hall is silent now. Some of the children look quite pale. Mrs. Chapman tells them not to worry.

Mrs. Chapman says she's sure they've heard other horrible things about head lice. But not all of them are true. For a start ...

Mrs. Chapman adds that head lice can't fly, jump, or swim, but they can crawl from hair to hair. This is how they spread from person to person, especially if your heads are close together.

Poppy and her class go back to their classroom. By now, everyone's head is itching. Even Miss Lindsay is trying her best not to scratch.

Miss Lindsay hands out some letters. She tells the children to take the letters home and give them to their parents or caregivers.

The bell rings at the end of school. Soon, the classroom is empty.

At home, Poppy gives the letter to her mom.
It says that there's an outbreak of head lice at school.
The letter tells her how to check for head lice and nits.

Poppy's dad goes to the shop to buy a nit comb. It's a special metal comb, with lots of fine teeth. He also buys a big bottle of hair conditioner.

The best way to check for and get rid of head lice and nits is called wet combing.

WHAT YOU NEED:

- a nit comb
- hair conditioner
- a wide-toothed comb

WHAT TO DO:

1. Wash and wet the hair, and apply lots of conditioner.

2. Use a wide-toothed comb to get out any tangles.

3. Part the hair into small sections, one by one.

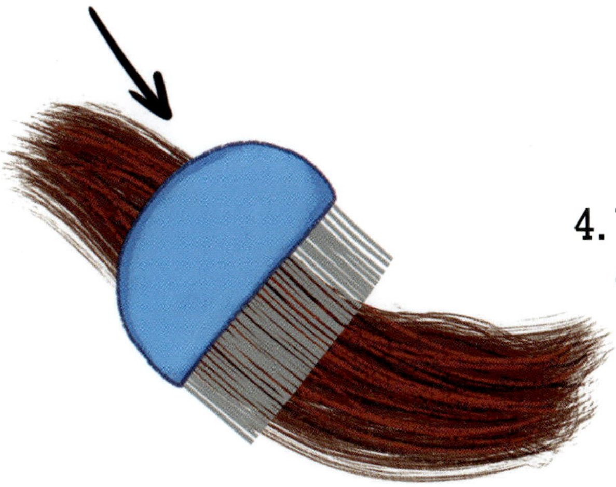

4. Use the nit comb to comb through each section from root to tip.

5. Each time, check the comb for head lice or nits. Wipe them on to a tissue and throw it away.

6. Check the whole head, then rinse off the conditioner.

Check carefully behind the ears and at the top of the neck. That's where head lice especially like to cling on.

Poppy's dad wet combs Poppy's hair. It takes a while because it's so long. Then he checks Poppy's brother's hair before checking his own. It's Poppy's mom's turn next.

Then Poppy's brother has a thought.

Poppy and her family need to wet comb their hair every four days for the next three weeks to make sure the head lice are gone.

After that, they all need to wet comb their hair once a week to make sure there aren't any more. There's nothing you can do to stop yourself from getting head lice. But if you check your hair regularly, you can find them and get rid of them early.

Back at school, Poppy and her friends chat about what they did over the weekend.

But they don't put their heads so close together anymore!

They all laugh. Having head lice isn't fun but anyone can catch them. And hopefully, they're all on their way to getting rid of them!

Then, suddenly, Jan starts scratching his head...

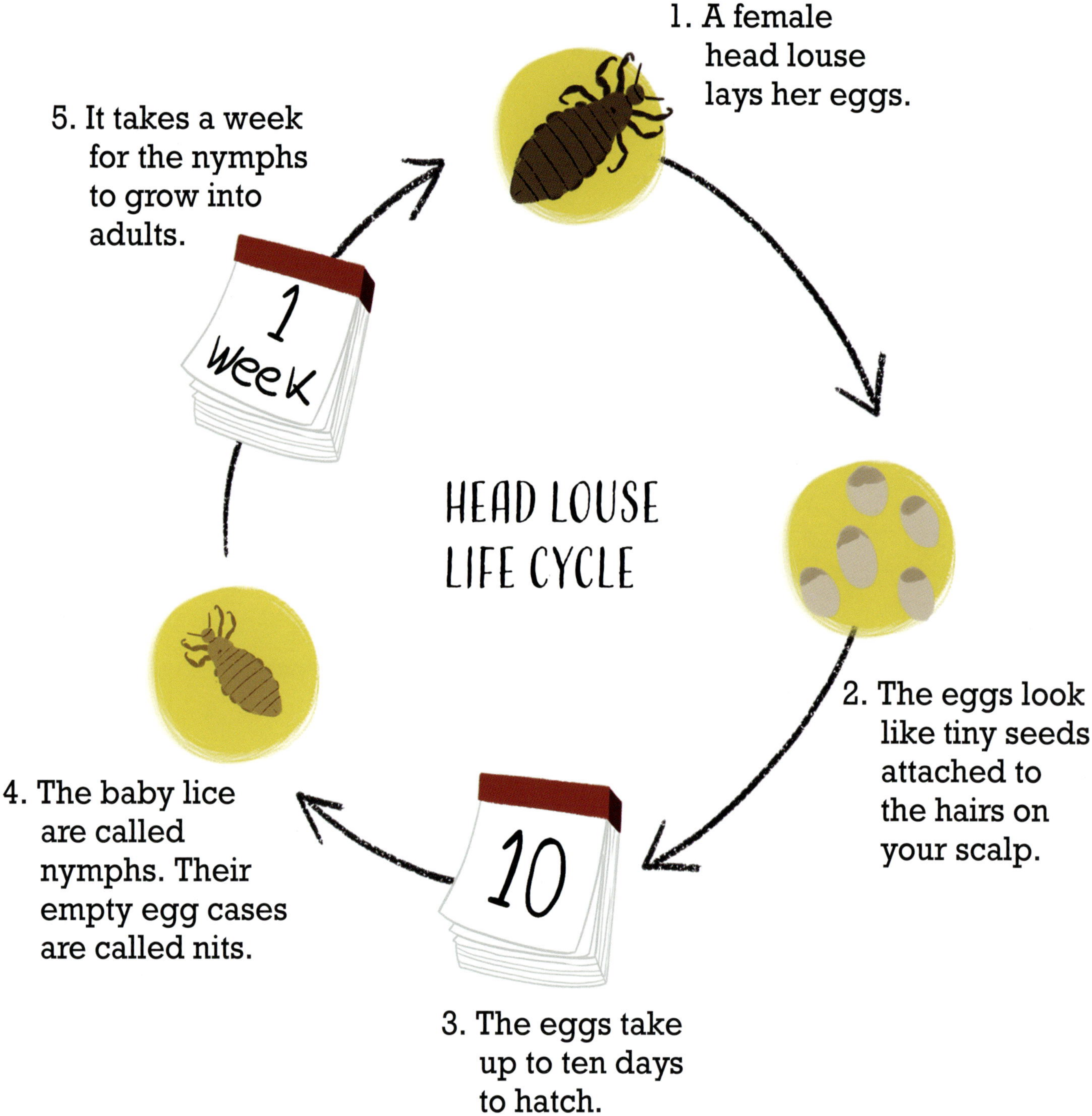

- Adult head lice live for about 30 days. In that time, a female can lay up to 300 eggs!
- Head lice are transparent until they have fed on blood. Then they turn a red-brown.

QUIZ

Now that you've reached the end of the book, how much do you think you know about head lice? Try this quick quiz to find out.

1. What kind of animal is a head louse?
a) a reptile
b) an insect
c) a fish

2. How big are adult head lice?
a) the size of a sesame seed
b) the size of a pea
c) the size of a grain of rice

3. Where do head lice lay their eggs (nits)?
a) in a nest
b) on your hair
c) in the ground

4. What kind of hair do head lice like?
a) clean hair
b) dirty hair
c) long hair

5. What is a nit comb?
a) a comb for getting rid of nits and head lice
b) a comb used by head lice
c) a comb shaped like a head louse

Answers:
1. b); 2. a); 3. b); 4. all of them; 5. a)

ADVICE FOR PARENTS AND CAREGIVERS

LOTIONS AND POTIONS

There are all sorts of medicated lotions and potions for treating head lice, and it can be difficult to know which one to choose. Only think about using them if wet combing hasn't removed all the head lice after doing it regularly for three weeks.

Ask your pharmacist for advice about which lotion to use, and how to use it correctly. Don't use lotions to prevent head lice - only to treat them.

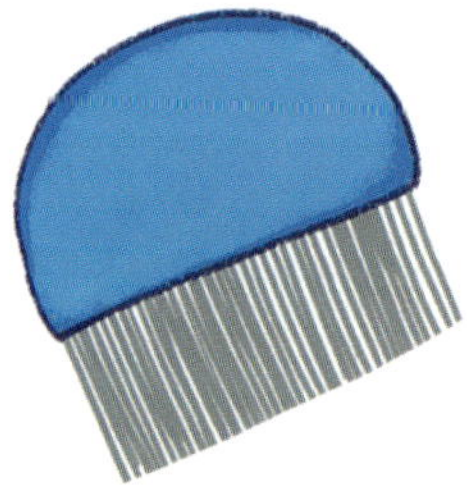

USEFUL WORDS

conditioner
Thick liquid you put on your hair after you have washed it.

fleas
Small, jumping insects that feed on human and animal blood.

head lice
Tiny insects that can live on your hair. One insect is called a head louse.

medicated
Something that has medicine in it.

nits
Empty egg cases of head lice.

nymphs
Baby head lice.

pharmacist
A person trained to give out medicines in a hospital or drugstore.

scalp
Skin on top of your head where your hair grows.

transparent
Something that you can see through.

wet combing
Combing through wet hair.

MORE INFORMATION

www.nhs.uk/conditions/head-lice-and-nits/
All about head lice and how to treat them. Includes photos to help you to identify head lice.

kidshealth.org/en/kids/lice.html
Lots more information for you about head lice and how to get rid of them.

kidshealth.org/en/parents/head-lice.html
Lots more information for your parents about what to do if you've got nits.

www.chc.org/for-parents/
This handy video will show you how to wet comb your hair for head lice.

BOOKS

All About Head Lice by Megan Borgert-Spaniol (Super Sandcastle, 2018)

Head Lice Drink Your Blood! by Natalie Humphrey (Gareth Stevens Publishing, 2024)

INDEX